T0380821

Sanctification Invitation

ANDREW C. CARTER

Photography by Megan E. Carter.

Scriptures taken from the Holy Bible, New International Version®, NIV®. Copyright © 1973, 1978, 1984, 2011 by Biblica, Inc.™ Used by permission of Zondervan. All rights reserved worldwide. www.zondervan.com The "NIV" and "New International Version" are trademarks registered in the United States Patent and Trademark Office by Biblica, Inc.™

WestBow Press books may be ordered through booksellers or by contacting:

WestBow Press
A Division of Thomas Nelson & Zondervan
1663 Liberty Drive
Bloomington, IN 47403
www.westbowpress.com
1 (866) 928-1240

ISBN: 978-1-9736-3660-1 (sc)
ISBN: 978-1-9736-3661-8 (e)

Library of Congress Control Number: 2018909765

Print information available on the last page.

WestBow Press rev. date: 12/07/2018

WESTBOW
PRESS®
A DIVISION OF THOMAS NELSON
& ZONDERVAN

also from Andrew Carter,

Sanctification Renovation

all photography in this book taken by Megan Carter

the author and photographer can be contacted via email at

sanctificationrenovation@gmail.com

in loving memory of

Grandma Fellin

whose spirit is forever present

The very first statement of the Bible is the boldest claim ever made. God (one supreme being) created the universe and everything in it. One chapter is all the Bible gives us to detail this process. Why not give more specifics? Why not elaborate on the intricacies of a flower or tell us why the sky is blue? Perhaps we could not understand. But why this casual, matter-of-fact account of creation? One of the most debated topics of all time, one that has perplexed humanity for centuries . . . simply stated- God did it. God wants us to know it is that simple. His statement as The Creator sets the tone for the entire Bible. Right up front. Either you have faith or you don't. If you can believe God imagined and formed everything...then you can believe God for anything. So, the question then becomes why not start there? Why not get this issue out of the way?

The man and his wife were both naked, and they felt no shame. Genesis 2:25

all the wonders of the world bestowed to one man

this was the genesis of God's plan

He also provided woman, the half that made Adam whole

but the crafty one slithered into a hole inside their soul

the very image of God wanted more

a seemingly insignificant choice ignited a great war

tranquility traded for tension- the world forever changed

God's only children suddenly estranged

humanity facilitated the manifestation of greed

the future was poisoned by this deadly seed

the soul now fertilized by doubt and pride

the first man born into sin yielded the blow by which his brother died

from *"no shame"* to *"only evil all the time"*

only one was found blameless, righteous and sublime

The Lord saw how great man's wickedness on the earth had become, and that every inclination of the thoughts of his heart was only evil all the time. Genesis 6:5

from no shame in the 2nd, to murder in the 4th, all but Noah gone in the 7th

by the 6th chapter of the Bible the *"Lord was grieved that he had made man" (Genesis 6:6)* and his wrath ensues

FaitHFuL aNd FLaWed-Step aSide aNd Let HiM be God

greatness and blessings were promised to him and his offspring
how could this man covet anything?
never before was more promised, never before was more required
eager to make it on his own, Abraham moved ahead of God to get what he desired
emboldened to father a great nation, doubt crept in
the seed of unbelief was growing within
Ishmael was Abraham's first but Isaac was the promised one
faithful to His word, God gave Abraham and Sarah a son
after all this, a test came from God
in this moment, Abraham proved more faithful than flawed
who could imagine such a request being made?
sacrificing his long-awaited son, the price to be paid
his voice must have been trembling, *"God himself will provide the lamb"* *Genesis 22:8*
Abraham's prayer was answered out of the thickets, the offering would be a ram
even the founding fathers of the faith struggled to rely on God
from Abraham to Joseph, they were faithful and flawed
perhaps drawing from the growing pains of his ancestors, Joseph describes a faith without flaw...
"I cannot ... but God will." Genesis 41:16

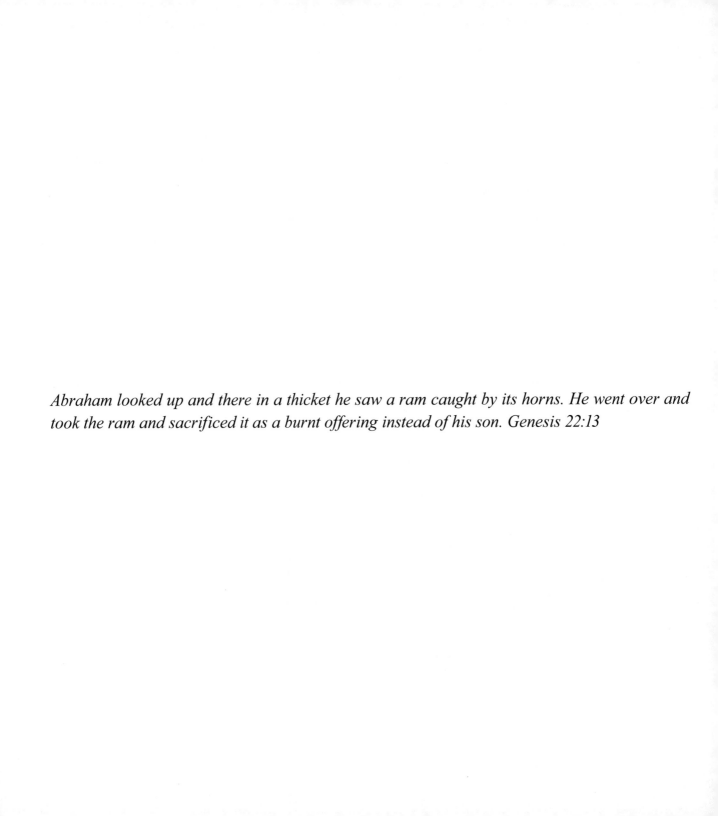

Abraham looked up and there in a thicket he saw a ram caught by its horns. He went over and took the ram and sacrificed it as a burnt offering instead of his son. Genesis 22:13

how quickly we forget, all the needs He has met

I will take you as my own people, and I will be your God. Then you will know that I am the Lord your God, who brought you out from under the yoke of the Egyptians. Exodus 6:7

follow the pillar - The Lord guides our path

this is our chance for freedom, to flee from Pharaoh's wrath

what more can our God do? how much more can He provide?

to prove His love for us? to show He's on our side?

the army is upon us, Lord hear our desperate plea

only One has the power to part the mighty sea

joy flooded our souls as we passed over the sea floor

but the majesty of the moment faded as we trekked on from the opposite shore

why does the miraculous become mundane?

once we've nothing more to gain

... "if only we had died by the Lord's hand in Egypt!" Exodus 16:3

you may not have been there to see the waters part

but the same Almighty God can fill the void inside your heart

somehow, He still provides for us even though we have the nerve to mock

we doubt that He could rain down bread or spring water from a rock

Exodus 17:2 ... "why do you put the Lord to the test?"

The Creator of the universe constantly second guessed

Moses answered the people, "Do not be afraid. Stand firm and you will see the deliverance the Lord will bring you today. The Lord will fight for you."
Exodus 14:13 & 14

do you stand out among your peers?
does the opinion of others paralyze you with fears?
set yourself apart
make it a matter of the heart
draw your line in the sand
your commitment to honor God's commands
not for a pat on the back
or your name on a plaque
but to know the glory of serving the Lord
forsaking this world to live on His accord
only you and God know where you should take a stand
proclaim His Name in this area and He will show you the promised land
how do you distinguish between the holy and the common?
if holiness was a crime, would you be arrested by the lawman?

You must distinguish between the holy and the common... Leviticus 10:10
If the Lord is pleased with us, he will lead us into that land... Numbers 14:8

I see the cloud moving but I'm standing still
a stubborn refusal to submit to His will
I must follow my faith to find freedom
the Spirit inside me that knows I need Him
the life God wants for me is waiting on the other side
He will lead me, let's go! – stop trying to hide
show me the way
I need You today
I want to see
Your glory in me
I'm inviting You in
take the place of my sin
no longer denied
come step inside
the realization of what could be
I give the best to You and refuse me

MOSES-THE CHOSEN ONE

Pharaoh tried to stunt Israel's growth through malice
but a Levite child born in secret floated up to the palace
The Great I Am called this man to lead
uncertain of his competence; intimidated indeed
the plagues, the Passover, the parting of the sea
Moses was the incarnation of the Lord's decree
deliverer of the original summons to sanctification
a call to live the Lord's way of life- a new declaration
discouraged by the grumbling of the Israelites
even the chosen one made costly oversights
through it all, one hallmark could not be ignored
Moses was a loyal steward of the Lord
an intercessor the likes of which the world had never seen
a man whose personal encounters with God were a normal routine

Moses is faithful in all my house. With him I speak face to face.
Numbers 12:7 & 8

time for a spiritual upheaval
purge the evil   *Deuteronomy 13:5*
our God is jealous
and we're rebellious
disposed to evil   *Deuteronomy 31:21*
but we're His people
called to strength and courage   *Deuteronomy 31:6*
assured to flourish
choosing evil
spiritually lethal
life and prosperity to gain   *Deuteronomy 30:15*
choosing ignorant disdain
The Lord our God is on the verge
am I the evil He will purge?

The Presence

THE PRESENCE OF GOD

RARELY SEEN,   ARMED FIGHTING MACHINE
EVER PRESENT   HOLY INTENT

IN THE SHADOW OF THE PRESENCE I FIND MY WAY
~~SHOULD I CEASE TO FOLLOW~~
                                      ASTRAY
THE PROMISES OF GOD SHALL NOT LEAD ME

                        I FOLLOW
THE SHADOW,   ~~THE PRESENCE,~~
~~GUIDES / MY WAY~~   SHALL NOT LEAD ME ASTRAY
GUIDES MY WAY   BE ~~IGNORED~~   NEVER STAGNENT
A CALL CANNOT   IGN~~ITED~~   GRAB YOUR SWORD
AN ENCOMPASSING FEELING   SWORD DRAWN
READY TO GO   IMPOSING THREAT
OBJECTIVELY REVEALING   THE CONCLUSION FORE
                            CONQUEST PRESET GONE

THE PRESENCE PROCLAIMS HOLINESS FOR ALL THE WORLD TO
                                                SEE
        WHEREVER IT MAY BE
ADVANCING THE AMBITIONS OF THE LORD

THE [ARMY OF THE LORD] IS [RECRUITING ~~THOSE~~
ONLY [THOSE WHO FEAR GOD] NEED APPLY

THE PRESENCE

rarely seen
ever present
armed fighting machine
holy intent
the shadow
an encompassing feeling
ready to go
objectively revealing
sword drawn
imposing threat
the conclusion foregone
conquest preset
the call cannot be ignored
join His squad
army of the Lord
recruiting those who fear God

Now when Joshua was near Jericho, he looked up and saw a man standing in front of him with a drawn sword in his hand. Joshua went up to him and asked, "Are you for us or for our enemies?" "Neither," he replied, "but as commander of the army of the Lord I have now come." Joshua 5:13-14

... as for me and my household, we will serve the Lord. Joshua 24:15

who will testify to what the Lord has done?
will you let the principals of God be overrun?
if you have witnessed His transforming power
you cannot afford to cower
as Christians, are we passing the test or passing the buck?
what is our response to pagans running amuck?
to kill those who promote evil may not be politically correct
as long as evil is tolerated, we will earn its effect
this is personal, not political
the support of the Lord could not be more critical
when our leaders have agendas of their own
our world will continue to resemble a combat zone
in this age of grace, there are lessons to be learned from the past
God will not tolerate evil; His judgement is steadfast
what will history say about our generation?
have we furthered the Christian Nation?

...another generation grew up, who knew neither the Lord nor what he had done for Israel.
Judges 2:10

when all seems lost . . . love will find a way
raise your hand, come on, take a stand
someone needs you,
someone needs you!
for the sake of the Lord, let you light shine bright
never give up the fight
this could be the moment- this could be the day!
glean love,
glean love!
spread love,
spread love!
someone needs that seed,
someone needs that seed!
even in the midst of a war,
at the bottom of the threshing floor
love will steal the show,
love will ever grow!
in the middle of the night,
the smallest glimmer of light will be-
all the hope you need,
all the hope you need!
to keep love alive,
keep love alive!
God is standing by,
God is standing by!
to flood another soul,
wash out all the old and be-
everything you need,
everything you need!

when all hope seems lost . . . love will find a way
never underestimate the power of the love of God
the most valuable resource of the people of God is a pure spirit of love

Where you go I will go, and where you stay I will stay. Your people will be my people and your God my God. Ruth 1:16

BE CAREFUL WHAT YOU WISH FOR

We want a king over us. Then we will be like all the other nations...
1 Samuel 8:19-20

somehow, we find a way
to be lead astray
God is very clear
yet we do not fear
we complacently stroll into His Holy Tabernacle - a story as old as time
we are somehow dignified even though our heart is covered with grime
it seems we will never learn
feels like the point of no return
again, and again
our pride leads us to sin
but with patience unheard of
His pride leads Him to love
enduring anything to come to our defense
this love defies common sense
though we willfully disrespect
for His sake, He will not reject

For the sake of his great name the Lord will not reject his people, because the Lord was pleased to make you his own. As for me, far be it from me that I should sin against the Lord by failing to pray for you. 1 Samuel 12:22-23

I am my own Goliath, feeding in to the giant
to the ways of the world I have become compliant
accustomed to saving face
rather than sharing grace
confronted by lies
I quietly compromise
but who is worthy of my fear?
the Lord God sees beneath my spiritual veneer
how do I proclaim His Name without alienating others?
in the melodrama of life, we are all sisters and brothers
the gospel is too great not to share!
yet I hide the good news from others, as if I don't care
to be willing to sling that stone
standing up for God, even if I'm all alone
may my faith arise ever more fervent
so that one day I may hear Him say, *"well done, good and faithful servant."*
Matthew 25:23

Man looks at the outward appearance, but the Lord looks at the heart. 1 Samuel 16:7

You are my lamp, O Lord; the Lord turns my darkness into light. 2 Samuel 22:29

filled with perversions and lust and the promise no one will tell
there's a shortcut to satisfaction that leads straight to hell
even you can be lead astray
and find yourself helpless prey
king David was just out for a stroll when temptation caught his eye
but don't be foolish enough to think, "I wouldn't be like that guy."
if this is your weakness, confess it to the Lord
if you have trampled your vows, beg to have them restored
a committed marriage is a powerful testimony
an offering to God, clothed in the blessing of matrimony
to honor your spouse is to honor the Lord
remember the time when she was all you adored
you would do anything to be by her side
thoughts of being together filled you with pride
the one girl who would change your life
and gambled on love too, to be called your wife
may we focus on "the one" like there is no other
a pure heart, the greatest gift to our lover
God does not take away life; instead, he devises ways so that a banished person may not remain estranged from him. 2 Samuel 14:14

... give your servant a discerning heart ... 1 Kings 3:9

may the prayer of those who seek the Lord forever be heard
may we not hesitate to call His Name whenever our spirit is stirred
may we have ears to hear when God is speaking *Matthew 11:15, Mark 4:9*
may the ways of Him be what we're wholeheartedly seeking
may our hearts also desire holy discernment
may our sinful ways be met with swift internment
may we be quick to confess when we've given in to sin
may we understand this battle is not if but when
may the Lord have an open hand when his servant reaches out
may the mercy of the Almighty never run out
may we always be humbled by all that God is
may we acknowledge the blessing to be called one of His
may our prayers promote hope to this dying world
may our faith save others– before God's wrath is unfurled

May the Lord our God be with us as he was with our fathers; may he never leave us nor forsake us. So that all the peoples of the earth may know that the Lord is God and that there is no other.
1 Kings 8:57 & 60

giving your sin an excuse …
letting Satan's demons loose
twisting the Word, looking for justification …
toxic to the whole Christian Nation
falling astray …
or leading the way?
another sad story …
or seeing the promised glory?
risking it all …
or having the courage to stand tall?
even the great king Solomon was seduced … is this really your alibi?
this type of perverted thinking is why Jesus had to die
cling to God's Word and pass up that momentary thrill
all of us can… but who will?
so many have failed
thus the Savior was nailed
all alone on the tree
Christ was tortured for you and for me

They followed worthless idols and themselves became worthless. 2 Kings 17:15
the chosen people of The Creator of the earth
foolishly wasted their worth
through spiritual compromise
wearing a religious disguise
behind closed doors or on high places
there was no shortage of sinful embraces
by the natives of the land they should have possessed
the people of God Almighty were oppressed
given in to the enemy's hands
lured away from the Lord's commands
but covenant renewals can stir up a generation
may we- at this time and place- be at the forefront of a spiritual renovation
let us surrender any spiritual slight
lest the Lord say, almost, but not quite
be it Asherah, Baal, celebrity or crown
may the people of God bring all the idols down
to see glory restored to the Christian Nation
may *"doing right in the eyes of the Lord"* be our only aspiration   *2 Kings 22:2*

For all the gods of the nations are idols, but the Lord made the heavens. Splendor and majesty are before him; strength and joy in his dwelling place. 1 Chronicles 16:26-27

heavenly topics leave us conflicted

by our own understanding, we are constricted

we set our own limits on what God can do

there is a ceiling on our faith He wants to break through

for His splendor and majesty have no bounds

our fear to follow has no grounds

surrender goes against our grain

we insist on ruling our domain

to be god of our own life- something we've all desired

a serpent's compromise we've all conspired

shall we submit completely and leave our life in God's hands?

or, take a few shortcuts to avoid certain "demands"

strength and joy are in His dwelling place

yet we are content continuing this rat race

we are destined to fail, Adam and Eve are in our DNA

everybody does it, what a trite cliché

open your mind today

that connection to God is one prayer away

all God has, all that He is

you can have the inheritance of a child of His!

© Megan Carter

As for the foreigner who does not belong to your people Israel but has come from a distant land because of your great name and your mighty hand and your outstretched arm- when he comes and prays toward this temple, then hear from heaven, your dwelling place, and do whatever the foreigner asks of you, so that all the peoples of the earth may know your name and fear you...
2 Chronicles 6:32-33

let it be known
don't go at it alone
the Glory of the Lord is where
I go to meet Him- in prayer
He hears, He sees
my fears, my pleas
I will meet you there- in prayer
my God is always there- in prayer
His glory
fills my story
I call upon His Name- anywhere
in prayer
an increase
in peace
I cast my care
when I humble myself- in prayer

Despite their fear of the peoples around them, they built the altar on its foundation and sacrificed burnt offerings on it to the Lord... Ezra 3:3

a new era of crusaders
in the rubble of Babylonia's raiders
outcasts in the Promised Land
such a departure from what God planned
forsaking their fear
with the candor of a seer
for the sake of following the Lord
to experience worship restored

NEVER TOO LATE
one believer
some would say an over-achiever
coming back to his roots
willing to get a little mud on his boots
persecuted but persistent
faithfully consistent
fulfilling promises
restoring prominence
the king's cupbearer Nehemiah
arose as his era's messiah
with the Word as his guide
a new covenant ratified
building walls and spiritual foundations
preserving hope for future generations
to be the cupbearer of Christianity to a lost soul
a worthy cause for which to enroll

Nehemiah 1:9

if you return to me and obey my
commands, then even if your exiled
people are at the farthest horizon,
I will gather them . . .

one believer
some would say an over-achiever
coming back to his roots
willing to get a little mud on his boots
persecuted but persistent
faithfully consistent
fulfilling promises
restoring prominence
the king's cupbearer Nehemiah
arose as his generation's Messiah
with The Word as his guide
a new covenant ratified
building walls and spiritual foundations
preserving hope for future generations
to be the cupbearer of Christianity to a lost soul
a worthy cause for which to enroll

if you return to me and obey my commands, then even if your exiled people are at the farthest horizon, I will gather them . . . Nehemiah 1:9

What can we, at this time and place, gain from Israel's history? King after king, uprisings and downfalls.

Every nation, every generation, every family, everyone. We all have a part in God's story whether we believe in and follow God or not.

When we each take inventory of our place in history we must consider the eternal. Something, somewhere- whether written, stated or depicted will define our life. For some people this means books are written and movies are made to chronicle their journey. For others, maybe only a photo or memory will remain when they are gone. But rest assured someone, somewhere will have something to say when your name is brought up.

What will be said?

Will the record of your life be positive or negative?

Do you stand for what you believe?

Are you easily forgotten?

These questions should convict us to our core to make something out of our time on this earth.

So, what are you waiting for?

Pursue your passions and define your destiny.

not immune to pain
suffering is not in vain
what can I do?
hope in You, trust in You
pleased but not pardoned
self-righteous hearts become hardened
friends pour salt
insisting it's your own fault
brought down low with no alibi
only to see clearly You are on high
what can I say?
my ignorance is on full display
the workings of our own mind we cannot comprehend
how much more the whole earth and all that's within
reliance on our own wisdom is flawed
if you want to keep score, don't play games with God

Though he slay me, yet I will hope in him... Job 13:15
... my witness is in heaven; my advocate is on high. Job 16:19
I know that my Redeemer lives... Job 19:25
The fear of the Lord- that is wisdom, and to shun evil is understanding. Job 28:28

Blessed is the man who does not walk in the counsel of the wicked or stand in the way of sinners or sit in the seat of mockers. But his delight is in the law of the Lord, and on his law he meditates day and night. He is like a tree planted by streams of water, which yields its fruit in season and whose leaf does not wither. Whatever he does prospers. Psalms 1:1-3

through my eyes- this is my world
seeking truth- I see blurred lines
seeking wisdom- I see brilliant philosophy
seeking righteousness- I see excuses
seeking love- I see selfishness
seeking acceptance- I see compromise
seeking joy- I see a mirage
seeking God- I see purity
seeking God- I see my faults
seeking God- I see purpose
seeking my heart, what does God see?

The Lord looks down from heaven on the sons of men to see if there are any who understand, any who seek God. Psalm 14:2

I must confess
my unrighteousness
guilt in my heart
keeps us apart
I know this is real
faith beyond how I feel
in that quiet moment
own it
guilt melts into humility
credibility

I acknowledged my sin to you and did not cover up my iniquity. I said, "I will confess my transgressions to the Lord"- and you forgave the guilt of my sin. Psalm 32:5

The Mighty One, God, the Lord, speaks and summons the earth from the rising of the sun to the place where it sets. Psalm 50:1

... wash me, and I will be whiter than snow Psalm 51:7

© Megan Carter

should this night last forever and I am hidden from your light
should I be blessed with the wings of eagles and be grounded from flight
should your Word lose its value because your servant stumbled
should the whole nation suffer to ensure I am humbled
as the quiet beauty of the moment is interrupted
gnashing of teeth permeates what I've corrupted
only you can mend what I have broken
salvaging hearts with love unspoken
by your mercy hope rises like the dawn
by your grace last night is foregone
as your servant recognizes evil and turns away
as guilt is called out and no longer allowed to stay
as fresh as the morning dew
my spirit is revived anew

Create in me a pure heart, O God, and renew a steadfast spirit within me. Psalm 51:10

"the bucket list"

behind home plate at the *World Series*

front row on BROADWAY

the peak of Mt. Everest

the beach on *Yasawa Island, Fiji*

an open gate to **righteousness**

may a spiritual journey be above and beyond all experiences
should we have the opportunity to enjoy such blessings,
may the Glory of God be the highlight of the trip

the gates of righteousness are open,
who will enter?

Open for me the gates of righteousness; **I will enter**... *Psalm 118:19*

as generations pass, so the wind blows
the hours and days we have, no one knows
hearts grow faint as man labors in vain
to witness such sorrow and pain
death seems the only relief
a pardon from grief
may we find within our spirit a reason to cope
anyone who is among the living has hope   *Ecclesiastes 9:4*
a revision for the American Dream
a content man reigns supreme
intricate as a game of chess
precious is the process
to find your sanctuary among the strife
gives meaning to everyday life
...there is nothing better for a man than to enjoy his work, because that is his lot. Ecclesiastes 3:22

Flowers appear on the earth; the season of singing has come, the cooing of doves is heard in our land. Song of Songs 2:12

The Lord Almighty has a day in store for all the proud and lofty, for all that is exalted (and they will be humbled) Isaiah 2:12

on that day
this life fades away
the proud will have no more to say
wisdom of the world humbled on that day
heart and soul prepare a way
so that I am ready on that day
all our sin is washed away
crimson turned white on that day
calling home all those led astray
returning to the shepherd on that day
my soul will fly away
eternal freedom on that day
give me a reason not to pray
for the dawning of that day
come what may
I am looking forward to that day

The arrogance of man will be brought low and the pride of men humbled; the Lord alone will be exalted in that day Isaiah 2:17

fear God

thinking I know better myself
I put Your Word on a shelf
knowing You give meaning to life
I trade sanctity for strife
the mention of Your wrath
should straighten my path
I tremble at the thought
afraid of getting caught
living for The Lord
may make others feel awkward
my fear is misplaced
I'm such a disgrace
instead of being respected
Your promises have been neglected
showing indifference to eternity
as if Your ways burden me
seeking the courage to see every moment impacted
Fear God, a creed enacted

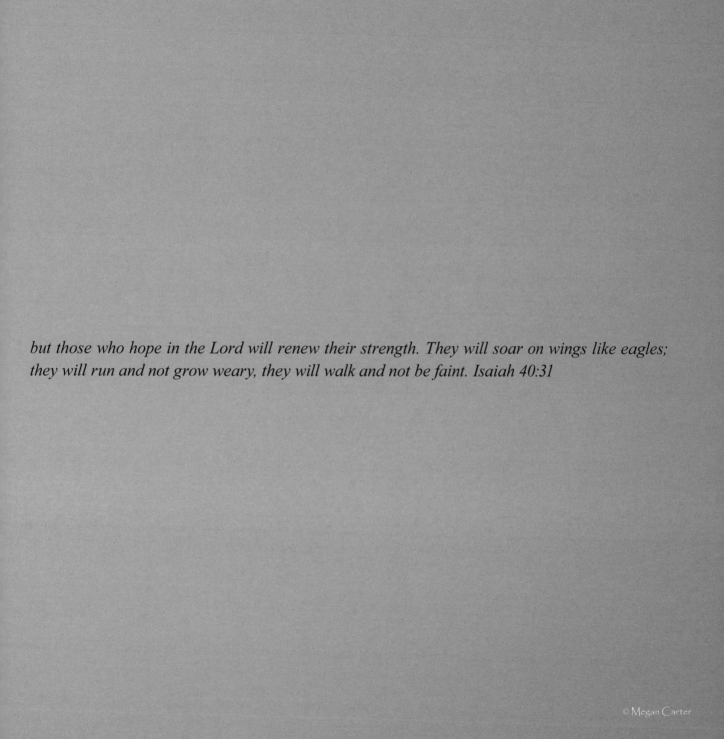

but those who hope in the Lord will renew their strength. They will soar on wings like eagles; they will run and not grow weary, they will walk and not be faint. Isaiah 40:31

"Should you not fear me?" declares the Lord. "Should you not tremble in my presence?"
Jeremiah 6:22

casual contempt
no lament
the blood is on our hands
we defiled Your commands
terror reigns throughout the city
The Sovereign Lord shows us no pity
for all to see . . .
the wrath of The Almighty
we strayed so far, The Father rejected us
a once proud nation declaring, "in God we trust"
for too many years we failed to repent
there's nothing to contest in His judgement

"Is it a trivial matter for the house of Judah to do the detestable things they are doing here? Must they also fill the land with violence and continually provoke me to anger?" Ezekiel 8:17

I gave them my decrees and made known to them my laws, for the man who obeys them will live by them. Ezekiel 20:11

explicit
intent
don't have to ask, don't have to guess
God's wisdom and power, I profess
the only reason I shine
the glory of His Spirit covers the darkness of mine
the only desire
faith on fire
bright as The Son
side by side with the 4th one
the symbol that quenches all doubt
His flame will never be snuffed out
holy incense
the presence   Daniel 3:25

If we are thrown into the blazing furnace, the God we serve is able to save us from it . . . but even if he does not . . . we will not serve your gods. Daniel 3:17-18

Blow the trumpet in Zion; sound the alarm on my holy hill. Let all who live in the land tremble, for the day of the Lord is coming. It is close at hand- Joel 2:1

they lie in wait
anxious to seal our fate
we carry on as if nothing's wrong
singing and drinking unaware it's our swan song
we ignore the trumpet sound
thinking someone's playing around
but in the midst of the party, a shrill cry pierces the sky - "alert the army,
the enemy's upon me!"
mayday! mayday! this is not a drill!
the soldiers are advancing upon our hill!
louder and louder the trumpet wails
laden by pride, our last-ditch effort fails
our calloused hearts we could not rend
a nation so torn apart only God Almighty can mend

When a trumpet sounds in a city, do not the people tremble? Amos 3:6
The Sovereign Lord will sound the trumpet Zechariah 9:14

At home alone or in a crowd, all I can think is how I wanna worship Your Name out loud. Daily life is forced interaction all for corporate gain. No one wants to shed their mask, we've all learned how to hide our pain. You pass someone, flash a smile, maybe say, "hello", might ask, "how's it goin?" But do you really want to know?

Don't let Jesus die in vain. Praise Him by making sin your greatest pain. Don't beat Him down again, lift Him up in praise. If you had to physically beat a helpless man before you committed a sin, how would your actions change? One thing I am tormented by, my sin caused Jesus Christ to die. How could I torture the King of Kings? That's the haunting reality each day brings.

What's your weapon- spear, thorn or nail? With which will you leave The Savior impaled? I think, "I'm a good person, that's not me." But my "little compromises" hung God on a tree. *Father, forgive me, I know not what I do. (Luke 23:34)* I so carelessly dismiss the pain I caused You. You died for me anyway. You accepted everything I did that day. Bleeding and bruised, You still offered me mercy and grace. I want to thank You Lord but I'm too ashamed to show my face.

Your power shook the ground and tore apart the veil of separation. A symbol of the barrier broken between The Creator and His Creation. Once again, God displayed His might. Darkness could not contain The Light. Death could not contain Him and He rolled away the stone. He rose to take His rightful place on the right hand of God's throne. The sin was overshadowed by the glory. Culminating in the climax of God's story.

I must overshadow my sin by the Glory of God.

Enter through the narrow gate. For wide is the gate and broad is the road that leads to destruction, and many enter through it. But small is the gate and narrow the road that leads to life, and only few find it. Matthew 7:13-14

angelic simplicity
devoid all mystery
unlocking the eternal
the key to this journal
seeking first
welcoming the worst
evil all around
sanctuary to be found
one of the few
to enter through
outlook grim
illuminate Him

all is given, all is required
everything needed, everything acquired
living on faith, living on a miracle
believing The Messiah, believing an oracle
for the sake of "sinners", for the sake of The Savior
forsaking reward, forsaking favor
never refused, never rejected
always loved, always accepted
willing to join, willing to be
able to lose, able to die on a tree
knowing The Father, knowing The Son
thy kingdom come, thy will be done   *Matthew 6:10*

Whoever acknowledges me before men, I will also acknowledge him before my Father in heaven. But whoever disowns me before men, I will disown him before my Father in heaven. Matthew 10:32-33

Further Benefits of Wisdom

3 My son, do not forget my teaching,
but keep my commands in your heart,
[2]for they will prolong your life many years
and bring you prosperity.
[3]Let love and faithfulness never leave you;
bind them around your neck,
write them on the tablet of your heart.
[4]Then you will win favor and a good name
in the sight of God and man.
[5]Trust in the LORD with all your heart
and lean not on your own
understanding;
[6]in all your ways acknowledge him,
and he will make your paths straight. [b]
[7]Do not be wise in your own eyes;

Walking with God

riginal Hebrew, "in all your ways
dge him" is more literally "in all your
him." This fundamental statement
ate to God implies more than
e. Nodding in God's direction is
must know him by living
elating to him person-
life.

© Megan Carter

If you believe, you will receive whatever you ask for in prayer. Matthew 21:22

do you not understand?
the Son of Man elaborates on the commands
He desires mercy
they want controversy
to be precise
Jesus became our sacrifice
indignant of His glory
opponents become accusatory
the power went to their head
the leaders conspired to see Him dead
the title meant to mock was indeed true
this is Jesus, The King of The Jews
the son of the only One good
He drank the cup no one else could

you must obey them and do everything they tell you. But do not do what they do, for they do not practice what they preach. Matthew 23:3

Holy Spirt confirmation
40 days temptation
fishing for men
driving out sin
authoritative teaching
prosperity preaching
compassionate healing
identity concealing
fellowship with "sinners"
divinely appointed dinners
attracting miracle seekers
aggravating rule keepers
making demons reform
calming storms
if anyone has ears to hear, let him hear   *Mark 4:23*
the wisdom of the kingdom of God is here

Others, like seed sown on good soil, hear the word, accept it, and produce a crop- thirty, sixty or even a hundred times what was sown. Mark 4:20

he's a rebel, a traitor!
he's The Messiah, Son of The Creator!
"Hosanna!" a triumphant hymn
"blasphemer, crucify him!"
have him arrested, have him killed
his life is prophesy fulfilled
save yourself, come down from the cross
the sacrificial lamb must pay the full cost
it's a scam, he's a fraud
"surely this man was the Son of God"   *Mark 15:39*
trembling with fear
He has risen! He is not here   *Mark 16:6*
the question to the Twelve, is also presented to us
who is Jesus?

"But what about you?" he asked. "Who do you say I am?" Mark 8:29

"*Glory to God in the highest, and on earth peace to men on whom his favor rests.*" *Luke 2:14*

Consider the ravens: They do not sow or reap, they have no storeroom or barn; yet God feeds them. And how much more valuable you are than birds! Luke 12:24

© Megan Carte

the climax to The Story
the climax to history
it was Jesus
it will always be Jesus
His life and purpose He tried to explain
His stories and claims only furthered their disdain
with boldness never seen
He drove a wedge in-between
challenged by the very people He came to save
in this world, to sin we are a slave
in word and deed, He was the Son of God
how could this man not bring confusion to a world so flawed?

I tell you the truth, anyone who has faith in me will do what I have been doing. John 14:12

believe
and receive
a new Way to live
repent and forgive
lead by the Spirit
while others fear it
the establishment feared a riot
but they could not keep quiet
healing the lame
but not for fame
locked in jail
an angel provided bail
their most worthy acclaim
to suffer for the Name
unashamed
and untamed

Now, Lord, consider their threats and enable your servants to speak your word with great boldness. Acts 4:29

let it be known
let Him be known
proclaim God's name
proclaim Jesus' name
Jesus, Savior
Author, Creator
God's Son, the Risen One
Messiah, revive us
engage us
to be courageous
Holy Spirit stir our soul
until our love is out of control
for You, for Your Word
until everyone has heard

One night the Lord spoke to Paul in a vision: "Do not be afraid; keep on speaking, do not be silent." Acts 18:9

not a loophole
but a foothold
an explanation
to the foundation
a guideline
to keep straight our sightline
a sinner is saved by grace   *Ephesians 2:8-9*
grace allows a sinful heart to be replaced
the new heart lives by the Spirit   *Galatians 5:25*
the Spirit knows the cost of disowning God and fears it   *Matthew 10:32-33*
the fear of the Lord is the beginning of wisdom   *Proverbs 9:10*
wisdom in the Word is spreading His kingdom
His kingdom will never end   *Luke 1:33*
the end of sin and death is a barrier we can transcend
to transcend this life is to live as Christ
Christ's righteousness was everyone's sacrifice   *Romans 5:18*
to live is Christ and to die is gain   *Philippians 1:21*
our gain was justified by His pain
from His pain, we gained eternal life
eternal life is perseverance through strife

And hope does not disappoint us, because God has poured out his love into our hearts by the Holy Spirit, whom he has given us. Romans 5:5

69

If you confess

with your mouth,

"Jesus is Lord," and

believe in your heart

that God raised Him

from the dead,

you will be saved.

Romans 10:9

nothing apart from Christ
the sinful nature will entice
everything the world has to offer
given away into the Lord's coffer
strengthened in service
let no man unnerve us
my weaknesses testify
Jesus' righteousness be my alibi
part of the perfect will of God   *Romans 12:2*
in this world, I'm flawed
so that it may be clear
to both foreigner and peer
may I be a reflection of God's glory
with the words of my story

God chose the foolish things of the world to shame the wise; God chose the weak things of the world to shame the strong. He chose the lowly things of this world and the despised things- and the things that are not- to nullify the things that are, so that no one may boast before him. 1 Corinthians 1:27-29

what do you do
when the Spirit gets ahold of you?
no turning back
from Satan's attack
gotta hold on
'till temptation's gone
ignorance was bliss
now I can't remiss
I belong to the Lord
this cannot be ignored
dead to sin
the Spirit is within
Christ is alive
in His service is where I thrive
I shed my scarlet letter
'cause now I know better
captivated by the Spirit
heaven help me should I smear it

God is faithful; he will not let you be tempted beyond what you can bear. But when you are tempted, he will also provide a way out so that you can stand up under it. 1 Corinthians 10:13

live as if you do

don't just say it but believe it's true
Christ is in you
faith without belief
is like Christmas without a wreath
if you don't have it, how can you show it
if you don't show it, how will others know it
the Good News cannot be spread
while you're living as if you're dead
the Word is life
the Word gives life
meet God halfway, where your faith joins with His power
believe it has happened and it will be yours at this very hour

Remember this: Whoever sows sparingly will also reap sparingly, and whoever sows generously will also reap generously. 2 Corinthians 9:6

When an evil spirit comes out of a man, it goes through arid places seeking rest and does not find it. Then it says, "I will return to the house I left." When it arrives, it finds the house unoccupied, swept clean and put in order. Then it goes and takes with it seven other spirits more wicked than itself, and they go in and live there. And the final condition of that man is worse than the first. Matthew 12:43-45

fill the void
of that impure desire that once annoyed
evil will return
crossing the bridge you didn't burn
fiercer than ever
more cunning and clever
Satan himself lacks nothing to incite
masquerading as an angel of light   *2 Corinthians 11:14*
when temptation's minions I cannot avoid
Holy Spirit fill the void
let them return to find
this house redesigned
in the places darkness hides
Christ now resides

Live by the Spirit, and you will not gratify the desires of the sinful nature. Galatians 5:16

what if it's today?
what if He's coming this way?
to call His children home
to take them as His own
where will I be found?
if I'm still around
living for His will
or chasing sinful thrill
what an awful sight
in the middle of the night
the Lord passes by
in the twinkling of an eye
brilliant as a shooting star
collecting believers near and far
the loneliest place on earth
disgracing your Christian worth
the day of the Lord will come like a thief in the night 1 Thessalonians 5:2

Brothers and Sisters of The Faith:

Glory to God for your spirit of sanctification pray the Creator of the sun, moon and stars be the sparkle in your eyes. May the words of the Lord written on your heart flow through everything you say. May your presence as a servant of Christ change the mood of every room you enter. May the full force of heavenly hosts protect your soul and guide your way. May you, by the power of Jesus, the ressurected Son of God, impact this world [for] in the Lord's love [purpose]